THE SEARCH FOR
TUTANKHAMEN

JANE SHUTER

Acknowledgements

Photos

Ancient Art and Architecture Collection, page 5. Popperfoto, page 7. British Museum, page 9. Griffith Institute / Ashmolean Museum, pages 11, 13 and 17. Margaret Orr, page 18. John Frost Historical Newspaper Service, page 20.

Illustrations

Angus McBride (Linden Artists), page 16 middle. Denis Ryan, page 21 (illustrations on 'Goosebumps' books covers – reproduced by kind permission of Scholastic Ltd). All other illustrations by Roger Stewart and Nick Harris.

Heinemann is an imprint of Pearson Education Limited,
a company incorporated in England and Wales, having
its registered office at Edinburgh Gate, Harlow, Essex,
CM20 2JE. Registered company number: 872828

Heinemann is a registered trademark of Pearson Education Limited

OXFORD MELBOURNE AUCKLAND
JOHANNESBURG BLANTYRE GABORONE
IBADAN PORTSMOUTH NH (USA) CHICAGO

The moral right of the proprietor has been asserted.

First published 1998

08
12

British Library Cataloguing in Publication Data
A catalogue record for this book is available from the British Library.

ISBN 978 0 435 09647 2   *The Search for Tutankhamen* single copy

ISBN 978 0 435 09648 9   *The Search for Tutankhamen* 6 copy pack

Designed by M2
Printed and bound in China (CTPS/12)

CONTENTS

INTRODUCTION

BRITAIN

EGYPT

SECRET TOMBS

This book is about the search for the **tomb** of Tutankhamen, who was king of **Egypt** over 3,000 years ago. At this time, the Egyptians buried kings in a place called the **Valley of the Kings**, in tombs cut deep into the rock. The Egyptians believed that dead people came back to life, so they buried them with everything they might need when this happened. The tombs in the Valley of the Kings were full of treasure made from gold, silver and jewels.

MEDITERRANEAN SEA

N
W   E
S

THE DELTA

EGYPT

CAIRO

RIVER NILE

THE VALLEY OF THE KINGS

THEBES

| 0 | 125km | 250km | 375km | 500km |

Scale 1 : 12,500,000

1cm on the map = 125km on the ground

The Egyptians lived along the River Nile. The rest of Egypt was desert.

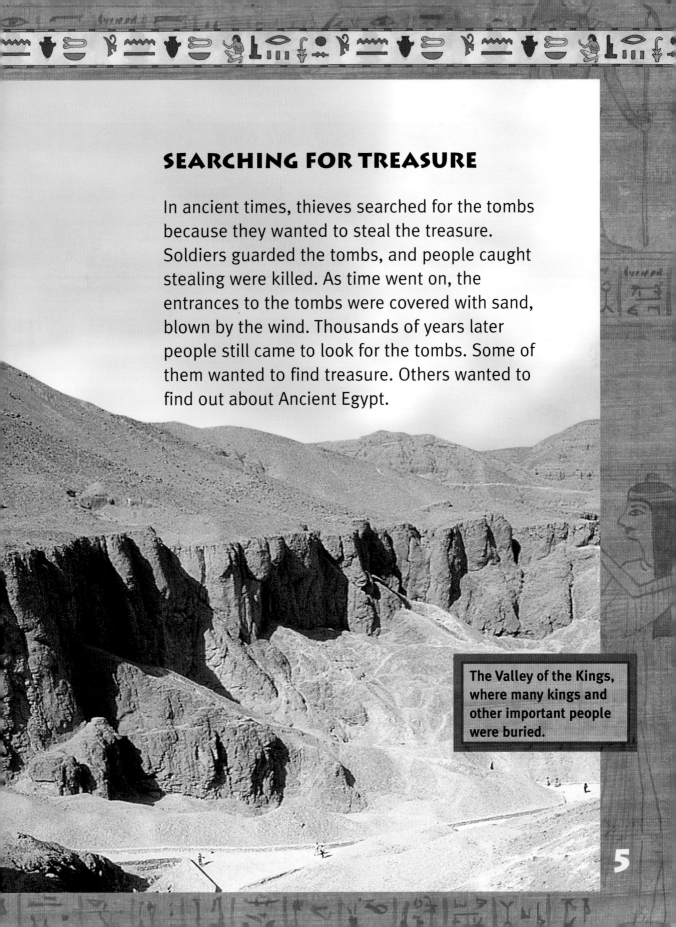

SEARCHING FOR TREASURE

In ancient times, thieves searched for the tombs because they wanted to steal the treasure. Soldiers guarded the tombs, and people caught stealing were killed. As time went on, the entrances to the tombs were covered with sand, blown by the wind. Thousands of years later people still came to look for the tombs. Some of them wanted to find treasure. Others wanted to find out about Ancient Egypt.

The Valley of the Kings, where many kings and other important people were buried.

THE MISSING KING

TUTANKHAMEN'S TOMB

By 1900, Tutankhamen was the only king buried in the Valley of the Kings whose tomb had not been found. Most of the **archaeologists** thought his tomb would not be discovered. Even if it was found, they said, all of the treasure would have been stolen many years before.

> People looked for the tombs of the kings over thousands of years. They hoped to find beautiful treasure, like this **mummy case** that held Tutankhamen's body.

TIMELINE OF EVENTS

1890	1895	1900	1905

1891 Howard Carter first went to work in Egypt, aged 17

1899 – 1905 Carter helped to excavate the Valley of the Kings

1907 Lord Carnarvon first went to Egypt and met Carter

THE ARCHAEOLOGISTS

Howard Carter was an archaeologist who helped to **excavate** the Valley of the Kings from 1899 to 1905. He was sure that Tutankhamen's tomb could be found.

Lord Carnarvon was a wealthy man who collected Egyptian treasures. He could afford to pay the costs of excavations, such as food, wages and equipment.

Carter and Carnarvon worked together to excavate the Valley of the Kings from 1914 to 1923.

Howard Carter

Lord Carnarvon

1910   1915   1920   1925

1914 – 1923 Carter and Carnarvon excavated the Valley of the Kings

7

PERMISSION TO DIG

WAITING

People had to get permission from the Egyptian government to dig in Egypt. Only one team of archaeologists at a time could dig in the Valley of the Kings. In 1907, Theodore Davis was already excavating the Valley of the Kings. Carter and Carnarvon had to wait.

DAVIS'S EXCAVATIONS

In 1907 Davis thought he'd found Tutankhamen's tomb, but when archaeologists cleared the tomb, they found it was not the right one after all.

From 1907 to 1912 Carter excavated other sites near **Thebes**. In 1913 he went to **the Delta**, another part of Egypt. His dig there was flooded, then invaded by cobras. There were so many cobras the archaeologists had to leave the site. Carter went back to Thebes.

A cobra on a royal crown. The cobra was the symbol for the Delta

A tomb painting of an Egyptian hunting in the Delta. The Delta is shown to be full of birds and fish. Cobras are not shown because painters were supposed to paint only good things.

CARTER AND CARNARVON BEGIN TO DIG

In 1914, Davis gave up his search, thinking there were no more tombs to find in the Valley of the Kings. Carter and Carnarvon got their chance. But the **First World War** broke out as they began to dig. Fighting in Egypt meant that they had to wait until 1917 to continue.

1910   1915   1920   1925

1914 Carnarvon and Carter got permission to excavate the Valley of the Kings

1917 Excavation began

SLOW BEGINNINGS

CARTER'S PLAN

Carter knew that the only way to find the tomb was to dig through the sand and rubble in the whole valley until he reached rock. It was the sensible thing to do, but it was slow work.

SIX HARD YEARS

Six years passed. By 1922 Carter had not found the tomb or anything valuable. Lord Carnarvon felt that he had given Carter large sums of money and had received nothing in return. Carnarvon told Carter to come to visit him in England to talk about this.

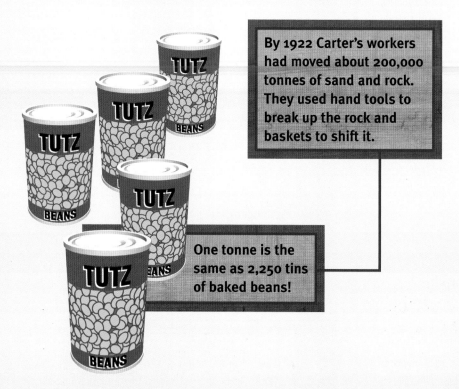

By 1922 Carter's workers had moved about 200,000 tonnes of sand and rock. They used hand tools to break up the rock and baskets to shift it.

One tonne is the same as 2,250 tins of baked beans!

ONE LAST CHANCE

In the summer of 1922 Carnarvon told Carter he would not pay for any more digs. Carter begged for one more year. He said that if they did not find anything, he would repay Carnarvon all the money he had spent that year. Carnarvon agreed and gave Carter one last chance to find Tutankhamen's tomb.

1910   1915   1920   1925

1917 – 1922 Carter excavated the Valley of the Kings, but found nothing

Summer 1922 Carnarvon told Carter to stop digging, but Carter begged for one more year

THE RIGHT TOMB?

A TOMB IS FOUND

Carter returned to Egypt on 1 November 1922 and began to dig again. Three days later, the workers found a step. The next day they cleared twelve steps. The steps led to a tomb, but they did not know whose it was. They went on clearing. A few days later, they reached a door with Tutankhamen's name on it. They saw that the door seal had been broken and re-sealed. It was the right tomb, but the archaeologists did not know if thieves had stolen the treasure. Carter sent for Carnarvon. They had to wait to find out.

THE TOMB IS OPENED

Carnarvon arrived on 24 November. Two days later the workers had cleared ten metres of tunnel to another bricked-up doorway. Carter took out some bricks. He lit a candle and looked through the hole. There was a long silence.

At last, Carnarvon asked if Carter could see anything. Carter said, 'Yes, wonderful things.'

6 November
Outer door found

26 November Door to the antechamber found and opened

November 1922 | 1 | 2 | 3 | 4 | 5 | 6 | 7 | 8 | 9 | 10 | 11 | 12 | 13 | 14 | 15 | 16 | 17 | 18 | 19 | 20 | 21 | 22 | 23 | 24 | 25 | 26 | 27 | 28 | 29 | 30 |

4 November
First step found

24 November
Carnarvon arrived in Egypt

The first sight of the inside of Tutankhamen's tomb. When Carter looked inside he saw 'everywhere the glint of gold'.

This drawing is of the bed in the photo, as Carter saw it.

1910   1915   1920   1925

1922

TUTANKHAMEN FOUND

THE ANTECHAMBER

When they got into the first room, called the antechamber, the archaeologists saw that it had been robbed. The thieves had probably been chased by guards. One of them had dropped a piece of cloth with some rings tied up in it. A door, guarded by two statues, led to the burial chamber. This had been broken into as well. It seemed that the thieves might have already found Tutankhamen.

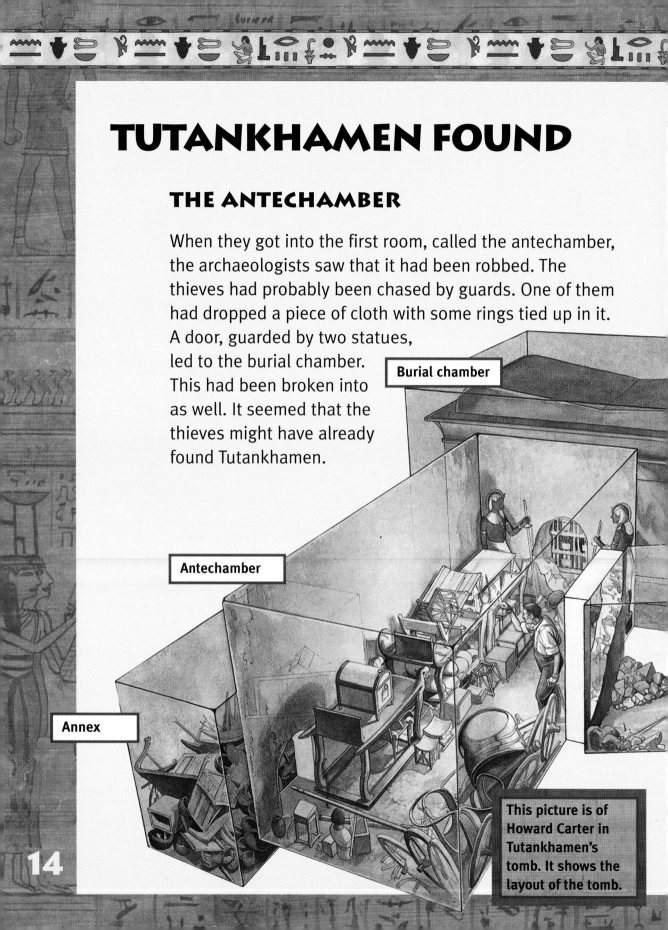

Burial chamber

Antechamber

Annex

This picture is of Howard Carter in Tutankhamen's tomb. It shows the layout of the tomb.

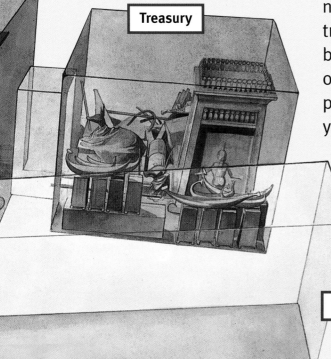

THE DEAD KING

When the workers opened the door, they saw that Tutankhamen himself had not been stolen. His body was still tucked away inside three mummy cases, a stone box and four wooden **shrines** covered in gold.

Treasury

Tunnel

MOVING ON

The archaeologists found that the tomb had four rooms, all crammed with treasure. Their next job was to sort the treasure and move it to safety, because once the news got out, thieves would be a problem again. It took several years to clear the whole tomb.

1910	1915	1920	1925

↑ ↑

December 1922 – February 1923
Treasures in the antechamber
sorted, packed and moved to safety

17 February 1923
Door to the burial
chamber opened

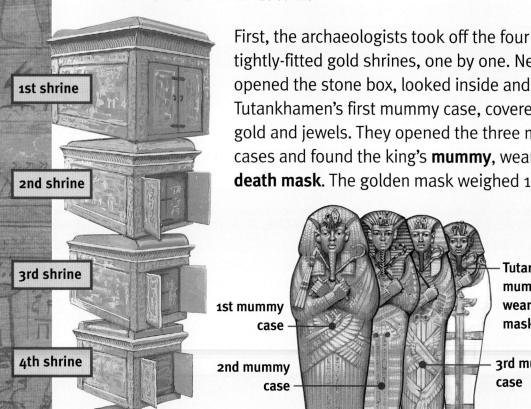

UNPACKING THE MUMMY

OPENING THE CASES

1st shrine

2nd shrine

3rd shrine

4th shrine

Stone box

First, the archaeologists took off the four tightly-fitted gold shrines, one by one. Next, they opened the stone box, looked inside and saw Tutankhamen's first mummy case, covered in gold and jewels. They opened the three mummy cases and found the king's **mummy**, wearing a **death mask**. The golden mask weighed 10.25 kg.

1st mummy case

2nd mummy case

Tutankhamen's mummy wearing death mask

3rd mummy case

10 October 1925 Work began on opening the mummy cases

November 1927 Work began on removing the treasures in the annex, the final room to be cleared

| 1923 | 1924 | 1925 | 1926 | 1927 |

March 1923 Work began on removing the shrines

28 October 1925 Tutankhamen's mummy reached

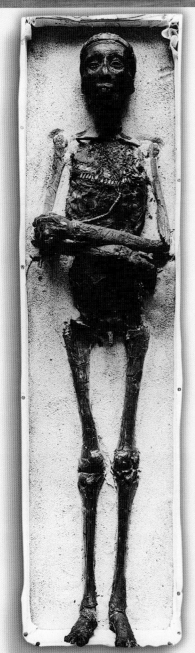

UNWRAPPING THE MUMMY

The archaeologists then unwrapped the mummy. They took off almost a thousand metres of linen strips. They tried to be careful, but the mummy was badly damaged. The head came away from the body, and the bones were broken in many places.

WHY WAS IT DAMAGED?

Historians aren't sure why the mummy was damaged. It might have happened because the archaeologists were not careful enough when they unwrapped the mummy, or it may be that the mummy was damaged because it was not properly **embalmed** before it was buried.

The unwrapped mummy of Tutankhamen.

1910   1915   1920   1925

PROBLEMS

VISITORS

The news of Tutankhamen's tomb and treasures brought visitors from all over the world. Kings, queens, archaeologists, historians and many others flocked to Egypt. They all wanted to look round. The archaeologists kept having to stop work to show people around the tomb.

A carved chair found in Tutankhamen's tomb.

Some famous historians who visited Tutankhamen's tomb. They are having lunch in the corridor of a nearby tomb. Howard Carter is second from the right.

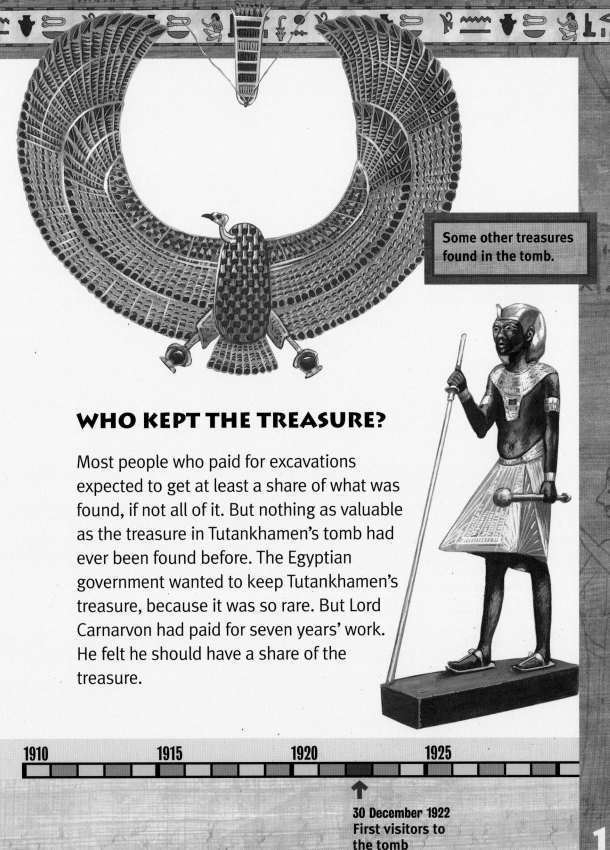

Some other treasures found in the tomb.

WHO KEPT THE TREASURE?

Most people who paid for excavations expected to get at least a share of what was found, if not all of it. But nothing as valuable as the treasure in Tutankhamen's tomb had ever been found before. The Egyptian government wanted to keep Tutankhamen's treasure, because it was so rare. But Lord Carnarvon had paid for seven years' work. He felt he should have a share of the treasure.

1910   1915   1920   1925

30 December 1922
First visitors to
the tomb

CURSED!

TUTANKHAMEN'S REVENGE

Lord Carnarvon did not live to argue over sharing the treasure. He died in **Cairo**, in 1923, when he caught an infection after being bitten by a mosquito. When he died, all the lights went out in Cairo. At the same moment, his dog, back in England, howled and died. The newspapers said Carnarvon's death was Tutankhamen's revenge for disturbing his tomb. By the next year, several people who had worked on the tomb had died mysteriously.

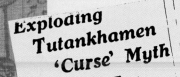

"CURSE" OF THE PHARAOHS.

TEN DEATHS OF TUT TOMB PARTY.

The ancient curse of the Egyptians—"Death shall come on swift wings to him that toucheth the tomb of a Pharaoh,"—was quoted once again yesterday when news reached England that a tenth person connected with the discovery of the tomb of Tutankhamen had met a tragic fate in the United States.

He was Dr. Jonathan W. H. Carver, who was killed in a motor smash at Columbus, Texas. His assistant, Mr. H. H. Miller, who was slightly injured,

Exploding Tutankhamen 'Curse' Myth

ALL ALIVE WHO SAW UNWRAPPING OF MUMMY

From Our Own Correspondent
NEW YORK, Friday.
Strenuous efforts to lay the ghost of Tutankhamen and to

TUTANKHAMEN'S CURSE AGAIN?

SCIENTISTS AND QUEER ACCIDENTS

From Our Special Correspondent
OXFORD, Friday.
"**D**EATH shall come on swift wings to him that toucheth the tomb of Pharaoh."
Once more the baneful influence of this curse of Ancient Egypt i

Curse Disproved
AMONG those who did most to disprove the belief that the

DEATH OF MR. H. CARTER

MAN WHO FOUND TOMB OF TUTANKHAMEN

"NEVER BELIEVED IN CURSE"

Mr. Howard Carter who, with the late Earl of Carnarvon, discovered the tomb of King

Some newspaper headlines about the 'curse' of Tutankhamen.

JUST A GOOD STORY?

Most people who worked on the tomb did not die mysteriously, including Carter and the man who unwrapped and studied Tutankhamen's mummy. Many people felt that if Tutankhamen wanted revenge, these are the people who would have died first. None of the Egyptians who worked on the site believed in the curse. But the idea of a mummy taking revenge was too good a story to leave alone. It has been part of films and story-telling ever since.

Some examples of modern stories that use the idea of 'the mummy's curse'.

1910   1915   1920   1925

↑
5 April 1923 Lord Carnarvon died in Cairo

1890	
1891	← 1891 Howard Carter first went to work in Egypt, aged 17
1892	

TIMELINE

1893	
1894	
1895	
1896	
1897	
1898	
1899	← 1899 – 1905 Carter helped to excavate the Valley of the Kings
1900	
1901	
1902	
1903	
1904	
1905	←
1906	
1907	← 1907 Lord Carnarvon first went to Egypt and met Carter
1908	
1909	
1910	
1911	
1912	
1913	
1914	← 1914 Carnarvon and Carter got permission to excavate the Valley of the Kings
1915	
1916	
1917	← 1917 Excavation began
1918	1917 – 1922 Carter excavated the Valley of the Kings, but found nothing
1919	
1920	
1921	
1922	← December 1922 – February 1923 Treasures in the antechamber sorted, packed and moved to safety
1923	←
1924	
1925	
1926	
1927	← November 1927 Work began on removing the treasures in the annex, the final room to be cleared
1928	
1929	

4 November 1922
First step found

6 November 1922
Outer door found

24 November 1922
Carnarvon arrived in Egypt

26 November 1922
Door to the antechamber found and opened

30 December 1922
First visitors to the tomb →

10 October 1925 →
Work began on opening the mummy cases

28 October 1925 Tutankhamen's mummy reached

GLOSSARY

archaeologist
a person who excavates places people have used in the past, to find out about them

Cairo
the most important city in Egypt

death mask
a mask put over the face of a mummy, painted to look like the dead person

the Delta
the marshy part of Egypt where the River Nile runs into the Mediterranean Sea

Egypt
a desert country on the African coast of the Mediterranean Sea

to embalm
to carefully preserve and wrap in strips of cloth

to excavate
to carefully clear away layers of soil to find out what is underneath

the First World War
a war that involved lots of countries and lasted from 1914 to 1918

historian
a person who studies the past

mummy
the preserved body of a dead person or animal, usually wrapped in bandages

mummy case
the painted, body-shaped wooden case that a mummy was buried in

shrine
a box or container, covered in holy pictures, usually with something precious inside

Thebes
a city in Egypt

tomb
a place where a dead person is buried

the Valley of the Kings
the place where the Ancient Egyptians buried many of their dead kings and other important people

INDEX